50p

THE REVOLUTIONARY PATH

D1741526

The Revolutionary Path

Moral Re-Armament
in the thinking of
Frank Buchman

GROSVENOR BOOKS, LONDON

PUBLISHED APRIL 1975 BY

GROSVENOR BOOKS

54 LYFORD ROAD, LONDON SW18 3JJ

ISBN 0 901269 14 X

© Copyright in Great Britain by The Oxford Group, 1975

The extracts from Frank Buchman's speeches quoted in this book are taken from *Remaking the World*, The Collected Speeches of Dr. Frank N. D. Buchman, published by Blandford Press, London, June 1961.

PRINTED IN GREAT BRITAIN BY
LONSDALE UNIVERSAL PRINTING LTD
SALISBURY ROAD, LARKHALL, BATH

CONTENTS

FOREWORD — vii

1. WHAT KIND OF CHANGE DO WE NEED? — 1
   Our primary need — 2
   A miracle of the spirit — 2
   The place to start — 3
   How to bring it about — 4
   Revolution to cure a revolution — 6

2. WE MUST REMAKE THE WORLD — 9
   Moral Re-Armament — 10
   The next step is revolution — 11
   Humanity at the crossroads — 16
   Chaos against God — 18
   There is an answer to crisis — 20
   The central revolutionary force — 22
   Remakers of the world — 25

3. IDEOLOGY FOR DEMOCRACY — 26
   The war of ideas — 27
   The only hope for world reconstruction — 32
   Which shall it be? — 36
   The full dimension of change — 40
   The revolutionary path — 42
   What we need is something electric — 46

4. FOR ALL MEN, EVERYWHERE — 48
   Bread, hope, peace — 49
   The new statesmanship to end confusion — 49
   The electronics of the spirit — 52
   The wrong way and the right way — 55
   Brave men choose — 60

FRANK BUCHMAN, BY PETER HOWARD — 65

FOREWORD

FRANK BUCHMAN set out on the path that led eventually to the world-wide action of Moral Re-Armament when his own life was radically changed in his early 'thirties.

The speeches from which the extracts in this book are taken began more than twenty years later when his work was already widely known, with visible effects in the lives of communities and even countries. They spring from living experience as well as from an original and questing mind. They span more than thirty years, from the emergence of the Oxford Group, as his work came to be called in the late 1920's, through the launching of the programme of Moral Re-Armament in 1938 and its expansion across the world, until his death in 1961.

These extracts try to bring out some of the central themes of Frank Buchman's thinking. Part of his genius was to make old truth new, and complex concepts simple enough for everyone to grasp. "Don't put the hay so high the mules can't get at it", he used to say. But it was the simplicity of a great mind, and he sometimes compresses into a single sentence what is really a whole philosophy of life or a new insight into some intractable problem.

His approach, so firmly rooted in practical reality and so wide in its horizons, added a new dimension to many people's concept of faith. He helped them to discover it as a revolutionary force affecting society, not only as a personal experience sustaining individual men and women. This was sometimes uncomfortable. Sometimes it aroused opposition. He challenged believers and non-believers alike to set out on a new road if they wished to bring an adequate answer to the issues of our time.

K.D. BELDEN

I

WHAT KIND OF CHANGE DO WE NEED?

IN THE YEARS before and after the First World War, Frank Buchman travelled widely in Asia. He became the friend of Mahatma Gandhi in India and Sun Yat Sen in China. He saw at first hand some of the revolutionary movements stirring the continents, and realised the inadequacy of the optimism and idealism of the post-war period. He tried to express the revolution he believed would be needed to create a new social order for which so many longed. He felt it must be a revolution which took into account not only the realities of war, hunger, poverty and tyranny in nations, but the reality of human nature in men. This was the key: to change men, to equip them with new aims and motives, and to enlist them in a programme of world change which would unite them above every division. As he travelled the world in pursuit of his aim, already defined in 1921 as "a programme of life issuing in personal, social, racial, national and international change", he sought to make these truths real in the lives of men. For to be effective they had to be lived, to be given legs, and such a radical change in human nature and in human society could come from one source only.

"The Oxford Group", he said, "is a Christian revolution, whose concern is vital Christianity. Its aim is a new social order . . . A new illumination can come to everyone and bring men and women of every creed and social stratum back to the basic principles of the Christian faith, enhancing all their primary loyalties . . . Upon a foundation of changed lives permanent reconstruction is assured. Apart from changed lives no civilisation can endure."

Our primary need

Human wisdom has failed.

The modern world—disillusioned, chaotic, bewildered—demands a solution adequate to its disorder.

The international problems of today are, at bottom, personal problems of selfishness and fear.

Lives must be changed if problems are to be solved. Peace in the world can only spring from peace in the hearts of men.

A dynamic experience of God's free Spirit is the answer to regional antagonism, economic depression, racial conflict, and international strife.

God-control is our primary need.

Geneva, January 1932

A miracle of the spirit

Today all Scandinavia is listening in to the broadcast of a Whitsun demonstration in the Castle of Kronborg, where the waters of Sweden and Denmark meet.

By a miracle of science millions can think and feel as one. Barriers of time and space are swept away.

We accept as a commonplace a man's voice carried by radio to the uttermost parts of the earth. Why not the voice of the living God as an active, creative force in every home, every business, every parliament.?

At the first Whitsun God spoke to a group of ordinary men. They changed the course of history. May He not today have a plan which can solve the problems of a troubled world?

The Holy Spirit is the most intelligent source of information in the world today. He has the answer to every problem. Everywhere when men will let Him, He is teaching them how to live.

The world needs a miracle. Miracles of science have been the wonder of the age. But they have not brought peace and happiness to the nations. A miracle of the Spirit is what we need.

Divine guidance must become the normal experience of ordinary men and women. Any man can pick up divine messages if he will put his receiving set in order. Definite, accurate, adequate information can come from the Mind of God to the minds of men. This is normal prayer.

There must come a spiritual dynamic which will change human nature and remake men and nations. There must come a spiritual authority which will be accepted everywhere by everyone. Only so will order come out of chaos in national and international affairs.

If this miracle is to come into the world some nation must give a lead. Some nation must find God's Will as her destiny and God-guided men as her representatives at home and abroad. Some nation must produce a new leadership, free from the bondage of fear, rising above ambition, and flexible to the direction of God's Holy Spirit.

Such a nation will be at peace within itself, and a peacemaker in the international family. Will it be your nation?

Denmark, Whitsun 1935
An address in the courtyard of Hamlet's
castle at Elsinore where 10,000 met from
Scandinavia and other parts of Europe

The place to start

Everybody wants to see the other fellow changed. Every nation wants to see the other nation changed. But everybody is waiting for the other fellow to begin.

The Oxford Group is convinced that if you want an answer for the world today, the best place to start is with yourself. This is the first and fundamental need.

Everybody admits the necessity of a moral and spiritual awakening. You find selfishness and fear everywhere—in men and in nations. One person really different. A million people different. A nation changed.

The secret is God-control. The only sane people in an insane world are those controlled by God. God-controlled personalities make God-controlled nationalities. This is the aim of the Oxford Group.

The true patriot gives his life to bring his nation under God's control. Such a nation will demonstrate that spiritual power is the greatest force in the world.

World peace will only come through nations which have achieved God-control. And everybody can listen to God. You can. I can. Everybody can have a part.

Will it be you? Will it be your nation?

Denmark, Easter 1936

How to bring it about

Leaders everywhere now say that the world needs a moral and spiritual awakening. They say it in the universities, in politics, in business and in chancelleries throughout the world. A lot of people say it—some in striking phrases. But it is still just *words*.

The problem is *how*. It is one thing to talk about it. It is another thing to demonstrate it. It seems to me that most people who feel the need for awakening are confronted with the difficulty that faced me twenty years ago: how to bring it about.

Now I find when we don't know how, God will show us if we are willing. When man listens, God speaks. When man obeys, God acts. The secret is God-control. We are not out to tell God. We are out to let God tell us. And He will tell us.

The lesson the world most needs is the art of listening to God. A general once sent me a postcard with the picture of a man on it. The thought below was this, 'God gave a man two ears and one mouth. Why don't you listen twice as much as you talk?' This is a daily possibility for everyone—to listen to God and get His programme for the day.

It is only necessary to obey the rules. The first rule is that we listen honestly for everything that may come—and if we are wise we write it down. The second rule is that we test the thoughts that come, to see which are from God.

One test is the Bible. It is steeped in the experience through the centuries of men who have dared, under Divine revelation, to live experimentally with God. There, culminating in the life of Jesus Christ, we find the highest moral and spiritual challenge—complete honesty, purity, unselfishness and love.

Another excellent test is, "What do others say who also listen to God?" This is an unwritten law of fellowship. It is also an acid test of one's commitment to God's plan. No one can be wholly God-controlled who works alone.

It is to a group of willing men and women that God speaks most clearly. And it is through God-controlled people that God must one day govern the world.

Birmingham, July 1936
addressing 25,000 people at an
Oxford Group demonstration in the
British Industries Fair building

Revolution to cure a revolution

I am speaking to you all from Europe where, hourly, news of revolution is coming in. It takes a passion to cure a passion. It takes a revolution to cure a revolution. And the Oxford Group's answer to revolution is more revolution—the revolution in human nature, which is our only hope.

What is this Oxford Group? Well, a newspaper man puts it in this way:

> It's not an institution,
>   It's not a point of view,
> It starts a revolution
>   By starting one in you.

The world today presents the spectacle of nations losing their way—of nations losing their traditions, their character, their nationhood. Many of us are blind to the haste with which events are hurrying on.

What is our real problem? You all know what a drought is. Well, we are suffering today from a spiritual drought. Fear and greed are like a dust storm. They spread over nations. They blind and choke people. They set man against man, class against class, nation against nation.

National and world problems remain the same because the root problem—human nature—remains unsolved. Until we deal with human nature thoroughly and drastically on a national scale, nations must still follow their historic road to violence and destruction.

Three thousand miles of ocean do not change this fundamental problem—and will not save us if we fail to solve it. The symptoms may differ in Europe and America. The disease is the same.

What is the disease? Isn't it fear, dishonesty, resentment,

selfishness? We talk about freedom and liberty, but we are slaves to ourselves.

The only possible alternatives today are collapse or God-control. And collapse is simply the selfishness of all of us together. Collapse or God-control. You and I, if we are selfish, are part of the disease; just as you and I, if we are God-controlled, can be part of the cure.

The Oxford Group is a revolution of God-control where God really guides you and your nation. Everyone is guided by something. What are you guided by? Is it your own desires? Is it your pocket-book? Your fears? Your wife? Your husband? Or what the neighbours think? If it is your own selfish plan, you are an enemy of the nation.

God made the world, and man has been trying to run it ever since. That must stop. You remember what Will Rogers used to say: 'God made man a little lower than the angels, and man has been getting a little lower ever since!' But now a new age has begun, where God is going to have right of way.

What we must have is a world-wide Christian front against the oncoming forces of materialism. We read of burning churches. The only answer to burning churches is a church aflame.

The god of efficiency is not enough. Goodwill and good works do not reach the heart of the trouble. Idealism has not succeeded. The truth is that any lasting social and economic recovery can only be built on the foundation of a moral and spiritual recovery.

A new illumination must come to the world. I knew the man who gave us electric light. Everyone can get light today provided he makes contact with the power station. And it is just as practical to make contact with God. God has illumination for us, if our contact is good.

The Oxford Group believes that it must be done not through one person, but through groups of people who have learned to work together under the guidance of God.

The Oxford Group believes that the ordinary person can do the extraordinary thing if he is in touch with God.

God can put thoughts into your mind. Have you ever listened for them? Have you ever tried taking pencil and paper, and writing down the thoughts that come to you? They may look like ordinary thoughts. But be honest about them. You might get a new picture of yourself. Absolute honesty, absolute purity, absolute unselfishness, absolute love. Those are Christ's standards. Are they yours? You may have to put things straight. I had to. I began by writing to six people, admitting that ill-will between us was my fault, and not theirs. Then I could really help people. Remember—if you want the world to get straight, get straight yourself.

Brains alone are not enough. It is obedience that counts —obedience to God.

God spoke to the prophets of old. He may speak to you. God speaks to those who listen. God acts through those who obey.

Suppose tomorrow morning you get up a bit earlier and try listening to God. Why not get the family to listen too?

We can listen in every day. If we do, and if we obey what we hear, it is conceivable that together we will usher in the greatest revolution of all time, whereby the Cross of Christ will transform the world.

London, August 1936
in a transatlantic broadcast

2

WE MUST REMAKE THE WORLD

By 1938 the world seemed to be moving inexorably towards another war. Hitler invaded Austria in the Spring, and his military ambitions were clearly boundless. To Frank Buchman the darkening world scene called for a mobilisation of the moral and spiritual forces of humanity. Men of goodwill everywhere needed a rallying point, a philosophy, a programme. Even if war became inevitable, such men and women would look beyond armed conflict to the work of reconciliation and reconstruction that must follow.

In this context the call for Moral Re-Armament was launched by Frank Buchman in 1938. It was a concept that caught people's imagination as it swiftly circled the globe. To Nazi Germany it appeared as "the Christian garment for world democratic aims . . . uncompromisingly taking up a frontal position against National Socialism". To many people in occupied countries it was the soul of resistance. To men and women in the forces of the Allied nations it was a source of strength and courage—and of hope that they could have a part in building the world they were fighting to make possible.

In peace or war, Frank Buchman's aim was undeviating: to create a world governed by the living God, a new society built on the foundation of changed men and women who would live for the world and for others, not for themselves.

Moral re-armament

The world's condition cannot but cause disquiet and anxiety. Hostility piles up between nation and nation, labour and capital, class and class. The cost of bitterness and fear mounts daily. Friction and frustration are undermining our homes.

Is there a remedy that will cure the individual and the nation and give the hope of a speedy and satisfactory recovery?

The remedy may lie in a return to those simple home truths that some of us learned at our mother's knee, and which many of us have forgotten and neglected—honesty, purity, unselfishness and love.

The crisis is fundamentally a moral one. The nations must re-arm morally. Moral recovery is essentially the forerunner of economic recovery. Imagine a rising tide of absolute honesty and absolute unselfishness sweeping across every country! What would be the effect? What about taxes? Debts? Savings? A wave of absolute unselfishness throughout the nations would be the end of war.

Moral recovery creates not crisis but confidence and unity in every phase of life. How can we precipitate this moral recovery throughout the nations? We need a power strong enough to change human nature and build bridges between man and man, faction and faction. This starts when everyone admits his own faults instead of spot-lighting the other fellow's.

God alone can change human nature.

The secret lies in that great forgotten truth that when man listens, God speaks; when man obeys, God acts; when men change, nations change. That power active in a minority can be the solvent of a whole country's problems. Leaders changed, a nation's thinking changed, a world at peace with itself.

'We, the remakers of the world'—is that not the thinking and willing of the ordinary man ? The average man wants to see the other fellow honest, the other nation at peace with his own. We all want to *get*, but with such changed leaders we might all want to *give*. We might find in this new spirit an answer to the problems which are paralysing economic recovery.

Suppose everybody cared enough, everybody shared enough, wouldn't everybody have enough ? There is enough in the world for everyone's need, but not enough for everyone's greed.

Think of the unemployed thus released for a programme of Moral Re-Armament; everyone in the nation magnetised and mobilised to restore the nations to security, safety and sanity.

Every man, woman and child must be enlisted, every home become a fort. Our aim should be that everyone has not only enough of the necessities of life, but that he has a legitimate part in bringing about this Moral Re-Armament, and so safeguards the peace of his nation and the peace of the world.

God has a nation-wide programme that provides inspiration and liberty for all and anticipates all political programmes.

Every employed and unemployed man employed in Moral Re-Armament: this is the greatest programme of national service—putting everybody to work remaking people, homes and businesses. A Swedish steelworker told me: 'Only a spiritual revolution goes far enough to meet the needs of men and industry.'

A Labour leader said: 'I have seen the Labour Movement triumph and felt in the midst of triumph an emptiness. The Oxford Group gave my life new content. I see in its message the only key to the future of the Labour Movement and of industry the world over.'

Only a new spirit in men can bring a new spirit in industry. Industry can be the pioneer of a new order, where national service replaces selfishness, and where industrial planning is based upon the guidance of God. When Labour, Management and Capital become partners under God's guidance, then industry takes its true place in national life.

New men, new homes, new industry, new nations, a new world.

We have not yet tapped the great creative sources in the Mind of God. God has a plan, and the combined moral and spiritual forces of the nation can find that plan.

We can, we must, and we will generate a moral and spiritual force that is powerful enough to remake the world.

London, June 1938
This speech on Frank Buchman's
sixtieth birthday, launched Moral
Re-Armament. He spoke in East Ham
Town Hall. Supporting him on the
platform were sixty East London mayors
and borough councillors. His call evoked
a world-wide response.

The next step is revolution

Today we want to forge a united battlefront. The clear issue is whether we are guided by God or not.

I hope that by the time I finish speaking some of you will have made a decision. We have come here with different objectives. First, some of the people have come here hoping to be changed. That is very good, very necessary. Some of you come here with the hope that you will learn to change others. That, too, is very necessary.

But the danger is that some of you want to stop there. I am tremendously interested in a third point—how to save a crumbling civilisation. That is the thing that interests me. But then I want a fourth thing. I want to reach the millions of the world.

All these things ought naturally to follow each other. If you are changed, you naturally want to change other people. The next thing is you want to save civilisation. Then you want to reach the millions out there. It is a natural programme.

But sin comes along. I don't know if you believe in it or not, but it is here. Don't spend the rest of the day arguing if it exists or not. That is what some of you would like to do. You would miss the whole point. We are not here to argue; we are here for constructive planning and action.

I know what some of you would like out of the Oxford Group—a nice comfortable awakening; you would call it a revival. A nice armchair religion. That is the thinking of some people. But if we stopped there, I should be sorry. If you stop there, I am your enemy unless I warn you. A person who has that conception today is not adequately thinking and planning to save the millions.

I am not interested, nor do I think it adequate, if we are going to begin just to start another revival. Whatever thoughtful statesman you talk to will tell you that every country needs a moral and spiritual awakening. That is the absolutely fundamental essential. But revival is only one level of thought. To stop there is inferior thinking. Unless we call for something bigger than that we are done for.

The next step is revolution. It is uncomfortable. A lot of Christians don't like the word. It scares them. It makes them goose-fleshy. That's where some of your critics come from—goose-fleshy Christians with armchair Christianity.

I know revolution makes people uncomfortable. I am not here to make you comfortable, and I am not here to make you like me. What the Oxford Group will give this and every nation is a spiritual revolution.

But some of you are not thinking this way. Some of the cleverest people in the world are thinking along the line of destructive revolution, and they are already at work. Unless we and others see the bigger vision of spiritual revolution, the other may be possible.

The point is this. Are the Christians going to build a Christian philosophy that will move Europe? Are you the kind of Christians who can build that revolution? Is that the New Testament? Is that Christian? Is that the sort of thing you are going to do? Is that your programme? Is that your policy?

If you are not going on that battlefront, I wish you well. I am not going to quarrel with you or criticise you. You do exactly what you like in the way you like. That's your idea of democracy.

I don't say it's true democracy, but it's the popular practice of democracy. For an increasing number of citizens in democratic states are now unwilling to acknowledge in speech and action those inner authorities on which the life of democracy depends. Each man has his own plan. It's so wonderful each to have his own plan. It's such freedom, such liberty! Everyone does as he pleases. But not in the Oxford Group. There you have true democracy. You don't do as you please, you do as God guides. You do God's plan.

I cannot go into all the qualities necessary for a revolutionary this morning. There were some people in the Acts and the Gospels who gave everything. There were others who did not give everything. Even in a revolution some people want an amount of padding around them. I want to ask you this morning whether you want to be that kind of a revolutionary. If so, there may be a comfortable place for you behind the lines. But somewhere on the battlefront we will have the real revolutionaries.

There is a third stage—renaissance. The rebirth of a people, individuals and the rebirth of a nation.

Can we have this rebirth of a man and nation? Some people do not like the idea of nations reborn, or of reaching the millions. They deride such a programme by calling it 'publicity'. It is amazing how many Christian people and otherwise clever people are put off by a thing like this. You mustn't get publicity when you want to build something! All the publicity must be for destruction—or must it?

Criticism is uncomfortable. I know that. I know what it means. But if you are a real revolutionary, you always maintain perspective, no matter what people say about you. No matter how stones come, you go straight ahead. Stones of criticism are so bracing—they just set you up for the day.

I thank God tremendously for what has been done in this place, for all the preparations you have made, for all the difficulties you have overcome. Grateful for all that, but let's remember there is still sin in the camp. And that sin may be inferior thinking.

You will do well today to read the fifty-first psalm. It is a tremendous human experience. And then read in the New Testament about the Cross of Christ. You will never, never, never come into this experience until you know the Cross of Christ. Some of you have heard about it, Sunday by Sunday, but it's not an experience. If it were experience, you would not shrink from anything.

I am going to promise you one thing. I am not turning back. I am not turning back, no matter who does, no matter what it is going to cost. I do not want you to come along just because I am here—that isn't it. That would be a poor revolution. That would be a poor fellowship. Let us for a moment see a picture of the Cross of Christ, and let me say, if you join in this great crusade, you will get the way of the Cross. I am not going to lure you by hopes of material success. I am not going to lure you by saying you are going to be heroes. I am not going to lure you, although I believe that these lands can give a pattern on how to live. It is a personal experience of the Cross. It is not I, but Christ. It is not I at the head, but Christ who leads.

There are meetings this afternoon—the lawyers, the educationalists. These are important, but there is another more important. Cancel all others if you must for this one— the meeting between God and yourself. The biggest thing this afternoon for you may be to go off alone and decide whether you are going to be one of these fellow-revolution-aries, where you are going to stand on this battlefront. I am not going to ask you to make a decision right now. The thing you have got to decide is between you and God. Do it alone. Write it down if you want to. It is a deed, like the transfer of property—so you turn over your life to God, for full and complete direction as a fellow-revolutionary.

Then you are going to be free. Then you are going to have true democracy because you are free. That's my challenge to you.

Visby, Sweden, August 1938
at a Scandinavian assembly where Frank
Buchman sought to widen the understanding
of those who were drawn to Moral
Re-Armament but had not yet grasped
its scope, or understood its aim of
bringing an answer to nations.

Humanity at the crossroads

I looked out on the fire of sunrise on the Jungfrau this morn-ing, as the Alps became illumined with the start of a new day. Is it to be God's light of a new day for Europe and the world; or is it to be the fading light of a doomed civilisation? The world faces this historic choice.

Immediate decisions lie with the few who hold the reins of history in their hands. Yet each of us must make the crucial decision that, come what may, our lives and our nations are to be controlled absolutely by the living God, and that we accept His plan for the world.

The Oxford Group is building a world organism that takes the needs of nations and answers them with men. It is a challenge to every man and every woman to enlist under God's control in that colossal task.

Humanity is at the crossroads. We must reach a final decision for ourselves and for our nations. Do we choose the road of selfishness that leads to uncontrollable violence and darkness? Or will it be the road of the Cross to a sound world, where we learn how to live together, where the ancient virtues of justice, understanding and peace rule under God over a sane humanity?

The choice rests with every man. For every man can under God be a remaker of men, and every God-controlled man becomes a force for Moral Re-Armament.

Is this conviction a passion in your heart? Then it will spread like fire through your nation.

Where are the men in every land who will rise and accept the sovereignty of the living God, who will fight for their nations now by enlisting under the King of Kings, and who will answer the aching hunger of mankind for peace and a new world?

Interlaken, September 1938
at the first World Assembly for Moral
Re-Armament, Frank Buchman under-
lined the basic choice facing humanity in
the hour of crisis.

Chaos against God

We are now fighting a greater war than any war since the world began. It is not nation against nation, but Chaos against God.

Valid religious experience has power to change a person, a home, an industry, a nation. Some expression of religious experience greater than ever before must be called into being, something unlimited by our prejudices, far above our personal points of view, something instinctively recognised by everyone as the long hoped for solvent of every problem.

We must rethink and relive our whole conception of religious experience. Much, admittedly, has not been valid experience. Oftentimes it has been religious invalidism—a crass, insipid, dull, tepid, unimaginative maladaptation of what ought to be great life-giving, nation-forming experiences. It has been a warped conception, marred by moral twists. Due to our spiritually poverty-stricken lives, we even glibly admit that business and politics do not mix with religion.

We have been so long on the low levels of religious experience that we cannot readily grasp what an Alpine range of experience could be ours if all our thinking, acting and planning were God-controlled and not man-controlled. We need a whole new creative force let loose in the world—a religious experience so dynamic, so wholly adequate that, in the words of Isaiah, 'Nations shall run unto thee because of the Lord thy God.'

Today we drift with the tide instead of creating the experience that will turn the tide. In the recent crisis many people again turned to God. Man's extremity may be God's opportunity. But as an Edinburgh landlady told me, 'It is one thing to pray during the crisis, as hundreds have done. It is another thing so to live that it does not happen again.'

Now, how can we find this new quality of living? How can we capture that spirit that can change the world? It can only come from a genuine religious experience—that is valid for a change of heart, for changed social conditions, for true national security, for international understanding. It is valid because it originates in God, and issues in actual changes in human nature.

Today one hears too much the voice of man. One is sated with it. One longs again for the Voice of God. Yes, longs for the Voice of God to become the voice of the people, the Will of God the will of the people.

Then a new spirit would sweep all countries, overcome all difficulties, bridge all points of view, conquer all prejudices, enhance all primary loyalties, and give unity to national life. A whole nation can respond to the great essentials. An Oxford shop-girl says, 'What England needs is a Magna Carta inspired by God and signed by everybody'.

To be valid in these decisive days, our religious experience must once again become a marching, fighting, conquering world force. A mighty change on a colossal scale is the only hope left. This change begins with a change in human nature through Jesus Christ.

New men—new homes—new industry—new nations— a new world.

The world is anxiously waiting to see what Jesus Christ can do in, by, for and through one man wholly given to Him—God-led. You can be that man.

The world is anxiously waiting to see what Jesus Christ can do in, by, for and through one nation wholly given to Him—a nation God-led. It can be your nation.

London, November 1938
a BBC broadcast in a series entitled
"The Validity of Religious Experience"

There is an answer to crisis

There is an answer to crisis and it must be made known.

Crisis shows our failure. Before crisis ends in catastrophe, have we the courage to face its real cause? We ourselves are the cause. It is the way every nation and every one of us has been living that has brought us where we are.

Every nation and every individual is responsible for the existing situation.

The failure lies not with one nation, but with all. We are all to blame. For in every nation those forces are at work which create bitterness, disunity and destruction. Nations, like individuals, have turned a blind eye to their own faults while pointing the finger at each other. Selfish men and selfish women make front-line trenches necessary. A wave of unselfishness sweeping through our nation and every other nation would be the permanent answer to war.

We have all wanted peace. We have sought it in pacts, in leagues, in alliances, in changes of systems, in economic and disarmament conferences, and we have sought in vain. We have wanted peace, but we have never paid the price of peace: the price of facing with God where we and our nations have been wrong, and how we and our nation, as God directs, can put wrong right.

A new spirit comes when we make an honest apology for our own mistakes instead of spot-lighting the mistakes of the other nation. There is a common meeting ground in the fact that we all need to change—nations as well as men. In a crisis of this kind, if leaders change, they can change their people. If people change, they can change their leaders.

The crisis is moral and can only be met in the spirit of Moral Re-Armament—the spirit of honesty, justice, and love. Moral Re-Armament means the power to change people—your enemies as well as your friends, the other nations as well as your own. We must be prepared for unexpected paradoxes.

Every man is responsible for his nation. Nations will make honest apologies and rectify past mistakes when the peoples of those nations demand that kind of national policy.

Each man has an immediate part to play. He can accept for himself a change of heart. He can decide to listen to God daily. He can start to build a hate-free, fear-free, greed-free world.

The sacrifice necessary for lasting peace is nothing compared with the sacrifice of war.

There is still time for a selfish, fear-driven world to listen to the living God. The forgotten factor in diplomacy is that God has an inspired plan for peace, and the means to carry it out through men and women who are willing to obey.

Above every other loyalty is loyalty to God. In obedience to the God of all peoples every nation will find its true destiny. This is the truest patriotism. It requires the highest courage. It gives the greatest strength.

We need now nation-wide thinking and action. We must point to the new era, the new type of personality, the new home, the new industry, the new type of government. During these days we must develop the framers of the just peace—the peace that will be permanent.

The future lies with the men and nations who listen to God and obey.

Boston, August 1939
in a broadcast to Europe and Asia

The central revolutionary force

I am speaking today to the millions across the world who in these anxious days are increasingly looking to Moral Re-Armament as the one hope for the future. Especially, I am thinking of the men in the front-line trenches, the men faced with the hard realities, the men who know what war is.

Yet where are the front-line trenches today? Today in many countries every civilian carries a gas mask, every garden has its air-raid shelter. It is a new phase in war, where everybody is responsible and every home is a front-line trench.

Our arts of reconciliation have not kept pace with the arts of war. The art of destruction is beginning to outpace the art of living. All our values are slipping as currencies slipped after the last war. As my friend the great Oxford philosopher, Dr. Streeter, said, "A race that has grown up intellectually must grow up morally or perish."

Today we have reached the parting of the ways. Civilisation, man-controlled, is faced with collapse. The long-endured cycle of moving from crisis to crisis must end. Nations must move beyond crisis to cure.

A new world philosophy is needed, a world philosophy capable of creating a new era of constructive relationships between men and nations. A new statesmanship and a new leadership will ensue from this heightened quality of thinking and living.

This world philosophy will emerge as people begin to get their direction from the living God. It will be within the framework of a hate-free, fear-free, greed-free quality of living.

Think of the cost of hate, fear and greed. Millions of men and women must carry gas masks today because men the world over have been living behind masks for years. Millions of men and women must grope through darkened cities because the nations have been living in a spiritual blackout. Millions of men and women today must listen to air-raid warnings because nations have not listened to the Voice of God in days gone by.

Times of crisis reveal the bankruptcy of our thought and action. Then we resort to feverish improvisation and expediency. Sheer economy of time and energy, and ultimate bankruptcy may force us to God-control.

Man today is ready to believe that human wisdom has failed. A situation is growing up in which people will want God to speak to them. They will have nothing else between themselves and desperation, as they read the changing, chimerical headlines that no one wants. Men need some adequate voice to interpret and mould events. Expediency must be supplanted by guidance. And dark nights of waiting may prove a blessing in disguise, for guidance is a staple necessity that is not rationed.

The world is awaiting an answer. War is the price of the selfishness of nations. We must have some simple, workable answer available for everyone, and one that can be applied by all. We need people trained not only to make an adequate peace, but also to keep it. Most people are selfish enough to want a peace that permits them to wage their own private wars and foster their own petty indulgences. An American housewife asks, "Who is responsible for the selfishness and greed in America today? Is it business, or labour? Or is it Mr and Mrs America in a million homes all over the country?"

Without the rise of a new spirit we shall pay heavily for our selfishness. An Army general said to me recently, "Either I sacrifice my selfishness for the sake of my nation, or I sacrifice my nation for the sake of my selfishness." And either we sacrifice our national selfishness for the sake of the world, or we sacrifice the world for the sake of our national selfishness.

The chief sin is that we have no adequate philosophy for

life. Our conception of living is wrong—easy, soft, protective, indulgent. We need a whole new content and conception of life. The brains and the thinking of the world must have been sabotaged and squandered for a very long time to create such destruction of men and nations.

We have tried thinking and living as we want. Now try thinking and living as God wants. Try living as we want the other fellow to live. Try living as we want the other nation to live. Then our nation will be the spearhead of a new world order.

MRA is the great central revolutionary force.

We are waging the greatest battle of history in this world war against selfishness. Every man to his guns! We must call out the moral and spiritual forces. We need to live a quality of life that will change masses of people. It is because we had no such adequate action during the last decades that we are compelled to make the costly sacrifice of war. The way to outlive the forces of destruction is to build better and more wisely than we are building now.

Our instant need is for millions to plan for the new world—not only a few statesmen meeting, but the united forces of the world backed by daily living and action that will support them in waging the eternal war against selfishness. Then we can begin to approximate to what is needed.

MRA is open to all and bars none. It is a quality of life. You don't join and you can't resign. You live a life.

The call is to everyone, the ordinary man and the statesman, unitedly to carry the burdens of their country. Responsibility has too often been delegated to the few in the belief that the statesmen is expected to do the thinking, planning and living that must become the concern of every man.

We must remake the world. The task is nothing less than that. Every man, woman and child must be enlisted, every home become a fort.

A world philosophy will be brought to power through the

cumulative effects of millions of people beginning the experience of listening to God. True, it may be only an initial experience. Enlistment does not immediately make the trained soldier, but we can all begin.

Now is the time to enlist for the duration in this world war against selfishness. We must be fighters ever!

We stand at zero hour on the threshold of a new world order.

San Francisco, October 1939
in a broadcast to Europe and Asia

Remakers of the world

May the Christ child bring us the birth of a new thinking at this Christmas time and usher in the new world that the statesman and every man wants. We need a fourth-dimensional thinking—a gift from God—that will lighten our darkness and bring a speedy answer.

Wise men came from afar, guided by a Star, at that first Christmas. May each one of us, illumined from afar, bring a gift to all mankind that will be more acceptable than any earthly reward.

Trials and tribulations are the furnace which forges prophets. May we have the courage to accept the gift of this fourth-dimensional thinking for which God has prepared us with a common unity of mind to become the remakers of the world.

Ours is the eternal unity of being guided by a Star to give to every man and the statesman the gift of a new world.

From a war-time Christmas message,
1940

25

3

IDEOLOGY FOR DEMOCRACY

As THE WAR went on, it became clear that the struggle was not only military but ideological. Victory in war would not, of itself, end this deeper conflict. If a new world of justice and harmony was to be built, something more far-reaching was needed by all nations, by victors and vanquished, by the democracies and the countries beyond what were soon to be called the iron and bamboo curtains. Frank Buchman began to give increasing emphasis to the need for the democracies to find an ideology of freedom which would go to the root of human need more effectively than materialism could do. The flaw in any materialist ideology is that it has, in the end, no way of dealing with human nature except by compulsion, terror or liquidation. It has in itself, therefore, the seeds of its own destruction. Moral Re-Armament points the way to a deeper revolution in the will and motives of men.

In the post-war years, Frank Buchman set out to apply these convictions, beginning in Europe, a continent in the throes of reconstruction. One need was to find a democratic road for Germany after the destruction of Nazism, and a basis for unity between nations once in conflict. This called for deep changes of attitude on all sides.

It was in these years that many Communist militants in the Ruhr, as well as in the north of France, northern Italy and elsewhere, found in Moral Re-Armament what they described as a more far-reaching revolution.

"Marxists are finding a new thinking in a day of crisis", Buchman could say in a broadcast from Gelsenkirchen in the Ruhr, in 1950. "The class struggle is being superseded. Management and labour are beginning to live the positive alternative to class war."

"Is change for all the one basis of unity for all?" he asked his listeners. "Can Marxists be changed? Can they have this new thinking? Can Marxists pave the way for a greater ideology? Why not? They have always been open to new things. They have been forerunners. They will go to prison for their belief. They will die for their belief. Why should they not be the ones to live for this superior thinking?"

In the same way he strove to further the rise of new attitudes in Japan, both in terms of democratic development and of reconciliation and reparation. The new relationships which came to be established between Japan and Korea, or the Philippines, as well as more distant countries like Australia and Holland, owed not a little to his work.

Frank Buchman had told his fellow workers thirty years before, "You must learn to think for continents." He did this consistently himself. Africa, Latin America, Asia, Australasia were ever present in his mind, as well as North America and Europe. His speeches, many of them given in the conference centres at Caux in Switzerland or Mackinac Island in America, reflect this daily preoccupation with the needs of distant peoples and of his friends among them.

The war of ideas

Today I want to talk about great forces at work in the world. Sixty and more years ago you didn't hear much about the Communist Party. To begin with there was one man—Karl Marx. Then for a long time only a small group. Eventually world conditions made it possible for Karl Marx to do his work—and Communism is the result.

Think what Russia means in the world today. How large

is it? One-sixth of the earth. I remember a time when the Czar couldn't ride unless he had every six feet a man watching him. Even if it was a railway journey of a thousand miles, he always had men posted along the way. It was all part of what helped produce the thing called Communism.

Today the Russians are doing pretty well. America is doing a lot for them because just now they seem to be a decisive factor in dealing with Germany, and because they may have a controlling interest in the future.

Now that is one picture. Give it a nice gold frame. Put in as much red as you want. But when you have done that, you haven't done with Communism because it is a tremendous force.

Now take another force. When did we begin to hear about Fascism? 1921-22. Again there was a man—Mussolini. I remember when I was in Italy, at Milan. *Viva i Comunisti* was written all over the walls. Soon you saw, *Viva il Duce*, also on the walls—and Mussolini arose as an opposing force to Communism. He marched on Rome. He put himself in power and a Fascist force came into being. For a while there was a growing sense of stability and prosperity. People said, "Good! Mussolini has come. Fascism has come. The trains are on time. There are no beggars in the streets. We have 'good order'."

But today where is Mussolini? Where is Italy? And where is the "order"?

In those days, back in the 'twenties, Germany was at its lowest ebb. Many had no food—nothing. For years there was danger of collapse and incipient revolution.

Then along came a man called Hitler who had very definite ideas. He wrote them in a book when he was in prison. When he came out there were mobs, disorders and massacres.

There was no order in Germany. But this juggernaut comes along and gives seeming order. More and more he took a place in the world. So the German people said, "Halle-lujah!" and *Heil Hitler!* You know the rest of the story.

So we have Communism and Fascism, two world forces. And where do they come from? From Materialism which is the mother of all the "isms". Materialism is Democracy's greatest enemy.

These then were the forces which threatened to dominate the world.

In 1938 the guidance came to me—"Moral Re-Armament", a movement where the moral and spiritual would have the emphasis. The need of the age is the moral and the spiritual. Our task was to bring these realities to nations that needed them. We initiated this thinking in London's East Ham Town Hall. We took it to the nations. MRA was born that year.

Communism and Fascism are built on a *negative* some-thing—on divisive materialism and confusion. Wherever Moral Re-Armament goes, there springs up a *positive* mes-sage. Its aim is to restore God to leadership as the directing force in the life of the nation.

America must discover her rightful ideology. It springs from her Christian heritage and is her only adequate answer in the battle against materialism and all the other 'isms'. But America does not hate materialism. Think of America de-stroying herself with the very force that she condemns in others. The battle of the ideologies was the granite of the Old and New Testaments. So many people today instead of giving the granite, give the sugar—and so we never cure materialism.

MRA first of all goes straight to the fundamental prob-lem—it recognises sin. Sin is the disease. Jesus Christ is the cure. The result is a miracle. You come to a training centre like this. You may say, "Oh, I don't like to hear sin men-tioned." Well, that's too bad. It ought to be mentioned, but it ought to be enough just to give a quick picture of it and then move on. And you ought to be so sensitive that you respond immediately and change—and that's one more miracle. That ought to happen today, just as in the old days your grandparents used to go to church on Wednesday night, because they liked a good rugged sermon on sin. That's fine if you have time for it—and possibly you need to take time. Make sure there is no minimum emphasis on sin. Make it maximum. But then quickly make the adjustment. Change, unite, fight. That is the natural sequence.

You will find here the old fundamental truths—but you get them with a mighty, moving crescendo. MRA restores absolute standards in a day when selfishness and expediency are the common practice of men and nations. Take the four absolutes—honesty, purity, unselfishness, love. Perhaps some of you do not put much stock in them any more. But to arm a people you must give them these simple, basic standards.

Take honesty for a start. What do you find in the nation? What about men who have been dishonest, say in war contracts? Graft and the Black Market keep a lot of people busy all the time and cost millions of dollars. In the old days nobody said a good word for dishonesty. Now the successful chiseller seems almost at a premium.

Take purity. You may say that it is just a personal matter. But what is happening to the nation? Too few try to bring a great, cleansing force to the nation. What is going to happen to a nation when nobody brings a cure any more? Broken homes, unstable children, the decay of culture, the seeding plot of revolution.

As far as unselfishness and love go, people don't pretend to be unselfish, and they don't expect to be loving.

People have written off the four standards as part of the horse-and-buggy days. So, naturally, they are the last thing they have in mind for nations. That is why you have the condition there is in the world today. Now if you can get people who will live up to these absolutes and stand for them, you have a force, a creative something in the community with a strength that nothing will gainsay.

You must have that emphasis on morals plus the saving power of Jesus Christ. Then you experience the dynamic which is almost forgotten—the Holy Spirit, that gives the guided answer and tells you exactly what to do as a clear direct call from God.

That's the programme for the Church today. I believe with all my heart in the Church, the Church aflame, on fire with revolution. We haven't begun to experience the spiritual revolution we need. You need revolution, and then when you come into the clear light of God's Presence, you will experience a glorious renaissance. You will come to see what Christ means this old world to be.

It's one thing to know these realities. But there's a further thing, and that is to make them national.

The trouble with some of you is that you are so idealistic that your hopes never come to pass, even in your own families. That was the trouble with the League of Nations. People were so 'League-minded' they failed to do the thing the League most needed—the spadework with individuals that brings change. There was something left out of the League and that was—God. The League was never God-arched.

Everybody's job is to find the God-arched master-plan. Then we would have a master-plan not only for us, but for post-war Europe. The trouble is, we let the statesmen do all our thinking for us—and then we call it democracy!

Take the great modern cities you come from. You complain of this subversive leader and that one. Yet it is the selfishness of everyone that makes possible the subversive leader. The whole problem is that you endure a thing rather than cure it. You would rather pay than pray. You would rather go on with your confusion, your grumbling, your complaints, than change and have an answer.

The battle for America is the battle for the mind of America. A nation's thinking is in ruins before a nation is in ruins. And America's thinking is in ruins.

People get confused as to whether it is a question of being Rightist of Leftist. But the one thing we really need is to be guided by God's Holy Spirit. That is the Force we ought to study. Then we will have a clear light that ends confusion. The Holy Spirit will teach us how to think and live, and provide a working basis for our national service.

America doesn't have much of her great moral heritage left. Just think, if we fail to give emphasis to a moral climate, where will our democracy go? Some of us have been so busy looking after our own affairs that we have forgotten to look after the nation. Unless America recovers her rightful ideology nothing but chaos awaits us. Our destiny is to obey the guidance of God.

The true battle-line in the world today is not between class and class, not between race and race. The battle is between Christ and anti-Christ.

Choose ye this day whom ye will serve.

Mackinac Island, July 1943
from an informal talk at a
North American Assembly

The only hope for world reconstruction

All the world wants an answer. We have reached the moment when, unless we find an answer and bring it quickly to the world, not just one nation, but all nations will be overwhelmed.

For too long we have breathed the atmosphere of problems. We move from conference to conference and give up hope of a fundamental solution. We are cynical of success. We have become the slaves of our defeats, personally and nationally.

Nations desire the fruits of an answer without having an answer. We want production. We want peace. We want prosperity. We want a world organisation. We want a united Europe. We want a new national life. But we do not go to the root of the matter.

You cannot continue to cry "Crisis" without providing an adequate answer. The habit of crisis breeds the habit of apathy. We must lift people to a new level out of the fogs of fear and the bogs of bitterness where today humanity founders.

Nations fail because they try desperately to combat moral apathy with economic plans. Economic breakdown walks as a black threat through the heart of every statesman and citizen. Yet the material crisis may obscure the materialism and moral breakdown that underlie it, so they do not know how to cure it.

Until we deal with human nature thoroughly and drastically on a national scale, nations must still follow their historic road to violence and destruction.

The problem is not just an iron curtain which separates nation from nation, but steely selfishness which separates man from man and all men from the government of God. And when men listen to God and obey, the steel and iron melt away.

A generation ago a group of men gripped by a materialist ideology decided to capture the world with it. They gave their lives to that task. For twenty-five years they have worked—every hour, sleeping and waking, ceaselessly, skilfully, ruthlessly on a world front.

Suddenly the statesmen of the democratic nations have

33

woken up. They rub their eyes as they see what is happening. The world force of materialism has penetrated every nation. It has infiltrated their schools, their industries. It has invaded their offices and government departments. It has influenced their families, their colleagues, and even themselves.

At last they realise the imminence of crisis. They perceive the colossal progress of organised materialism in its march towards world chaos and control. Why, they ask, are we in this situation? How did it come about?

The reason is simple. While many slept, and others busied themselves with their own affairs, the materialists have been working out their revolution with a philosophy, a passion and a plan.

What is the answer? A generation ago the force of Moral Re-Armament began fighting too. On a world front it has been answering plan with plan, idea with idea, a militant godless materialism with a militant inspired ideology for democracy.

The idea caught hold. It remade men. It impacted nation after nation. Now it girdles the globe.

Today at the Moral Re-Armament Assembly at Caux we see this force in action with the answer, available for service. At a time when statesmen realise the lateness of the hour, it freely offers the fruit of twenty-five years of toil. A force in the war of ideas, with the training and experience which, under God, can equip the statesmen and the ordinary man with an ideology adequate to remake the nations—now.

A new message goes out from Caux to a stricken world. At Caux the answer has been found. It has been given legs and it is on the march. Here at Caux we are reaching the end of the age of crisis and pioneering the era of cure.

A great Indian labour leader was with me at Caux last week-end. He told me two problems dogged India—racial bitterness and class bitterness. He saw no solution. After one day he told me he had seen the answer. He came again. He says: "Moral Re-Armament is the answer because moral apathy is the problem. I have seen here the way of life without tragedy. As I make this way my own, my life can be effective and I can make others effective. This is our chance. One of us can make many. Thousands can make millions. The world can be saved from tragedy."

His words are the key to statesmanship that can save the world. He shows us where to begin, because Moral Re-Armament is for everyone everywhere.

Human nature can be changed. That is the basic answer. National economies can be changed. That is the fruit of the answer. World history can be changed. That is the destiny of our age.

Let us be honest and face the facts. A new conference is no answer to a false philosophy. A new theory is no answer to a militant ideology. Plans fail for lack of inspired people to work them. Yet we multiply plans. Caux produces the inspired people who will make plans work.

A statesman came to Caux. He is President of the Board of Trade of his nation. For years life had been governed by a hatred of the British so powerful that he had sworn never to speak the English language publicly again.

He was involved in incidents which brought his country to a crisis that, in his own words, "could very easily have led to civil war." He spoke in English as he told us: "I have experienced myself that a hatred which at times used to flash to white heat can be removed in an instant through willingness, although I did not know God or believe in Him, to learn His miracle-working power." He learned the secret that an honest apology leads to honest peace. Civil war was averted. Change in this statesman and the guidance of God turned him from a divisive element in his nation to a pioneer of teamwork and taught him to live effectively for other races as well as for his own.

35

A change of heart. Inspired statesmanship. The answer we are all seeking?

Men born again are bringing renaissance to nations. Industry with this force of Moral Re-Armament at its heart will produce enough for the needs of all. Homes with this force in everyday life will secure the next generation from chaos. Armies with this force will give new standards of moral training to their nations. Cabinets and diplomats with this force will be totally effective for they will have the power to turn their enemies into friends. Europe will arise, the world will arise from the sleep and defeat of apathy and disillusion. This is the only possible hope for world reconstruction.

Caux, July 1947
an address at the opening of the second
World Assembly at the conference
centre at Caux, Switzerland, provided
after the war by the sacrifice of
hundreds of Swiss families.

Which shall it be?

Everywhere men long for peace and prepare for war. They long to rebuild and prepare to destroy. They plan for new prosperity and expect fresh disasters.

What is the missing factor in the planning and the statesmanship of the world today?

It is our lack of an ideology for democracy. We say, we are democrats, we need no ideology. We almost feel it is a sign of weakness to talk about an ideology.

So we try to meet the united plan and passion of alien ideologies with talk and with lip-service to high ideals and with a last resort to force. And we hope to live as we have always lived—selfishly, comfortably and undisturbed.

We have all lived too long in an atmosphere of imagining that security, prosperity, comfort and culture are natural to man.

We forgot the eternal struggle between Evil and Good, victory in which brings the blessings of security and prosperity. But defeat in this struggle, and even ignorance of it, brings poverty, hunger, slavery and death.

It takes more than diplomacy to exorcise evil. It takes more than lip-service to fight for God. Statesmen talk about the answer. They talk of union. But disunity increases. They talk of moral values. But immoral policies prevail. They use these words which the hard logic of events has proved true. But it remains words. These men do not face the cost in their own lives and the life of their nations of giving an answer.

An extreme of evil must be met with an extreme of good. A fanatical following of evil by a passionate pursuit of good.

That is why democracy fails. Only a passion can cure a passion. And only a superior world-arching ideology can cure a world divided by warring ideologies.

We Americans have been lulled into a false security by believing that all the "isms" are across the sea.

"Isms" grow from unsolved problems in the life of men and nations. One man's hate kindles a million hates. One man's suspicion explodes a million suspicions. It spreads like a prairie fire. Or it creeps like a flame underground to burst out unexpectedly in a hundred places.

Why is our record of broken homes so high? How about industrial strife?

Are we victims of the greatest "ism" of all—materialism?

Is materialism the mother of all the "isms"? Is materialism becoming our national ideology?

We stretch our generous hands to help Europe and Asia

37

economically. But materialism frustrates our best intentions. Prices rise, money is worth less. Troubles in industry cut down the supply of goods. At the moment when our strength is most needed abroad, we may find ourselves in our greatest crisis.

Ten years ago Moral Re-Armament was born. In this very Hollywood Bowl the crowds gathered to see the preview of a new world order.

What have we learnt in these ten years?

We have learnt that democracy without an ideology can win a war but cannot build a peace; that ideological preparedness is the task of the whole nation, and is the one sure basis of national strength, moral, military and economic.

Today MRA offers the democracies and the whole world the superior armament of an ideology, without which armies are out-fought and statesmen are out-thought.

MRA has grown in ten years to the stature of a world answer to any 'ism'—even materialism. It has restored for millions the simple sanctities of home and honour, and given hope for a new world. It has built the world organism that can make a reality of this hope.

One hundred and fifty leading Germans came to the World Assembly for Moral Re-Armament in Caux, Switzerland. General Clay in Berlin and Lord Pakenham in London made their visit possible. These Germans found the answer to nihilism and to an ideologically broken nation. A leading German Socialist, former Minister-President, said, "If Europe is to be saved, it must be saved in the spirit of Moral Re-Armament."

The first democratic handbook by Germans giving the answering ideology was produced by these men. It is going out far and wide even behind the Iron Curtain. Sweden gave 100 tons of paper because she saw her security lay in a new spirit in Germany.

French industry—battlefield of the ideologies—has

found a uniting force. An employer, heading an organisation of employers of 600,000 workers, fought Labour. The head of all the Socialist women of France mistrusted Management. These two saw the new battle-line—for or against democracy's inspired ideology. They met. They changed. They apologised, and are working together. Thousands rally to them. They speak not of revolution, not of reaction, but of renaissance—the rebirth of a nation, the rebirth of a continent.

Italy—focus of an anxious world. Two hundred Italians, including twenty-six Members of the Italian Parliament from five different parties, came to the MRA Conference last summer. The Christian Democrat and the Socialist learned to work together. A Socialist said, "It is a miracle. Our parties can get together in the same way as we have." Is that one of the secrets of the Italian elections?

What is the common factor in all this good news? It is *union*—the almost forgotten solution to all our problems today.

Division is the mark of our age. Division in the heart. Division in the home. Division in industry. Division in the nation. Division between nations.

Union is our instant need.

Division is the work of human pride, hate, lust, fear, greed.

Division is the trademark of materialism.

Union is the grace of rebirth. We have lost the art of uniting because we have forgotten the secret of change and rebirth.

Moral Re-Armament is the good road of an ideology inspired by God upon which all can unite.

Catholic, Jew and Protestant, Hindu, Muslim, Buddhist and Confucianist—all find they can change, where needed, and travel along this good road together.

God is calling men everywhere to be the instruments of

39

union. It comes not by conferences, not by laws, not by resolutions and pious hopes, but by change.

Change is the heart of the superior ideology.

As individuals change, a new climate comes to the nation's life. As leaders change, policies become inspired and the nation's life-blood flows again. As statesmen change, the fear of war and chaos will lift. The most difficult will respond to the firm, united but humble voice of reborn democracy.

Why should there be catastrophe again when, with God, renaissance is inevitable?

This is the new pattern of freedom for all nations. Shall it be a new Dark Age for Europe and the world? Or shall it be world-wide Renaissance of the moral and spiritual forces everywhere, bursting into life and bringing at the last moment a miracle to mankind?

Which shall it be? The decision lies in your hands.

Los Angeles, June 1948
on the tenth anniversary of
Moral Re-Armament

The full dimension of change

Moral Re-Armament has the tremendous uniting power that comes from change in both East and West. It gives the full dimension of change. Economic change. Social change. National change. International change. All based on personal change. It creates a personal opinion that can change the fate of nations. It presents a force adequate to remake the world. It shows how to unite nation and nation, and creates inspired democracy in families, industries, cabinets and nations. It is the inspired living that makes nations think and live. It has God's mind.

Karl Arnold, Minister-President of North Rhine-West-phalia, says, "The real answer to any ideology must be a superior ideology. Germany needs an inspired ideology to support her new democracy. Moral Re-Armament is the spiritual road to a new Europe. In our cabinet we have already begun to see the fruits of this ideology at work. This is the ideology which can bring us the moral and spiritual healing we need in our nation and provide a real basis of peace with other nations. When the nations of the world seek the good road with conviction and passion, then I believe there is a new beginning for the world."

His colleague, Minister-President Ehard of Bavaria, echoes his thought when he says of Moral Re-Armament, "This is what the world can be. This is what the world should be. This is what the world must be."

This works for everyone everywhere. What man wants is security—a hate-free, fear-free, greed-free world. The bottle-neck is that people say human nature cannot change. But human nature does change, and the nature of nations can change too.

Dr Hans Boeckler, Chairman of the Trade Unions of the British Zone, was at this conference. He says, "If men are to be free from the old and the outmoded, it can only happen as they set themselves a new goal, and place in the forefront humanity and moral values. I believe that Moral-Re-Arma-ment can bring about a definite improvement for mankind in many areas of life. When men change, the structure of society changes, and when the structure of society changes, men change. Both go together and both are necessary. The goal which Moral Re-Armament strives to reach is the same as that for which I am fighting as a trade unionist."

A French woman, Madame Laure, former head of the Socialist Women of France, replies, "I had good reason to hate Germany when I came to Caux. But a miracle hap-pened. When I found Germans who lived Moral Re-Armament, my hatred died. A common ideology is doing for France and Germany today what sentimentality never did between the two wars. Now we have this firm ground to stand on from which both sides are honestly striving to build the bridge of understanding."

Why is Moral Re-Armament the answer? Because it deals with the fundamental problem. A Mid-Western farmer said, "I used to wonder, when I read my Old Testament, when God stopped talking to people. When I met Moral Re-Armament I realised He hadn't stopped talking; people had stopped listening."

Someone has said that the modern man is not worried about his sins, but the result is that he is worried about almost everything else. Moral Re-Armament takes sin seriously. And it takes Christ seriously. Bishop Wurm of Germany writes, "In Moral Re-Armament people do not talk so much about the Cross of Christ, but they live by the power of the Cross of Christ. All come under its influence. That is why they can unite people of different parties, nations and confessions."

A labour leader sums it up: "Moral Re-Armament is not a new trade union. It is not a new religion. It is not a new political party. It is the remedy in the common fight for a new world."

Caux, June 1949
in a world broadcast

The revolutionary path

Twelve years ago I walked in the woods of the Black Forest near Freudenstadt. The world was on the edge of chaos. Just as today, everyone longed for peace and prepared for war.

As I walked in those quiet woods one thought kept

coming to me—"moral and spiritual re-armament, moral and spiritual re-armament. The next great movement in the world will be a movement of moral re-armament for all nations."

A few days later I was in London in the East End where the British Labour Movement began. The workers responded. Moral Re-Armament went to the world. The newspapers carried it, the radio. Today, twelve years later, in many parts of the world people are gathering to plan for the Moral Re-Armament of their nations. The London workers are meeting in Poplar Town Hall with the dockers. In Birmingham Town Hall labour and management from the British heavy industries and the coal-mines are celebrating the day, and in Glasgow the Clydeside shipworkers.

Messages have been coming in the last few days from Australia and New Zealand, from India, South Africa, America, from all parts of Europe, from Japan and the Far East.

What is the secret behind the triumph of a God-given thought? What is it that has enabled an ordinary man like myself, and hundreds and thousands of men and women across the world, to do the extraordinary thing?

Only the very selfish or the very blind person is content to leave the world as it is today. Most of us would like to change the world. The trouble is, too many of us want to do it our own way.

Some people have the right diagnosis, but they bring the wrong cure. They reckon without God and without a change in human nature, and the result is confusion, bitterness and war. Other people are quite sure they have the answer in theory, but they always want somebody else or some other nation to begin. The result is frustration and despair.

When the right diagnosis and the right cure come together, the result is a miracle. Human nature changes and human society changes.

43

Let me illustrate this with a personal word, because it happened to me one day forty-two years ago. For the first time I saw myself with all my pride, my selfishness, my failure and my sin. "I" was the centre of my own life. If I was to be different, then that big "I" had to be crossed out.

I saw the resentments I had against six men standing out like tombstones in my heart.

I asked God to change me, and He told me to put things right with those six men. I obeyed God, and wrote six letters of apology.

That same day God used me to change another man's life. I saw that when I obeyed God, miracles happened. I learnt the truth that when man listens, God speaks; when man obeys, God acts; when men change, nations change.

That was the revolutionary path I set my feet on forty-two years ago, which millions are treading now, and on which I challenge you to join me today.

What are you living for? What is your nation living for? Selfish men and selfish nations can drag the world to total disaster. A new type of man, a new type of statesmanship, a new type of national policy—this is our instant need, and this is the purpose for which Moral Re-Armament has come to birth.

A young Swiss engineer, successful in his profession, with family, friends, position and wealth, died this spring. He had discovered this same secret of investing his life and his possessions to create a new world based on change. He gave himself with his wife, who is with us today, and with his children, to make Caux the world centre it has become for all nations. Suddenly people have realised that in five short years he accomplished more for the world than many men in their whole lives.

This young Swiss followed in the steps of another young man who, seven hundred years ago, put aside fame and career and gave everything he had to change the world.

He brought a new life to Europe and his life has inspired countless millions since then. He was St. Francis of Assisi. This young Swiss engineer, so his wife tells me, kept constantly by him these words of St. Francis; and they are the secret of how to change the world:

> Lord, make me the instrument of Your peace.
> Where there is hatred may I bring love;
> Where there is malice may I bring pardon;
> Where there is discord may I bring harmony;
> Where there is error may I bring truth;
> Where there is doubt may I bring faith;
> Where there is despair may I bring hope;
> Where there is darkness may I bring Your light;
> Where there is sadness may I bring joy.
> O Master,
> May I seek not so much to be comforted as to comfort,
> To be understood as to understand,
> To be loved as to love;
> For it is in giving that we receive,
> It is in losing our lives that we shall find them,
> It is in forgiving that we shall be forgiven,
> It is in dying that we shall rise up to eternal life.

Gelsenkirchen, June 1950
at a reception, attended by hundreds of
Ruhr miners and their families, at which
Dr. Buchman was invested with the French
Legion of Honour for his contribution to
better understanding between
France and Germany

What we need is something electric

What we need is something electric—a shock that brings men and nations to their senses before it is too late. Something powerful enough to weld unity out of the hardest elements.

I remember the first electric light. It revolutionised our living. It altered men's thinking about the future. Is there today a discovery that can go into every home in every nation and unexpectedly bring an answer to our darkest problems?

A man from Washington came to see us. At the end of the evening he said, "I and my experts discuss everything except the point. Moral Re-Armament deals with the point". Next morning he got up early and telephoned to his superior in Washington. He apologised to him for a resentment against him which he described as the deepest resentment of his life. He said on the telephone, "What is the use of us talking to the world about unity when we have division right here in our own offices in Washington? I was self-righteous. I have not been fully honest with you. I am sorry."

Everyone everywhere can make contact with the source of power and illumination that changed the thinking of the man from Washington and told him what to do.

The short-circuit is human selfishness. It breaks contact. It is the source of darkness and loss of direction. When selfishness is crossed out, every home and every Cabinet can be power stations radiating an answer that works.

We are in the midst of the breakdown of our civilisation —war in the home, war in industry, war between the nations. What is the future? Further disintegration, chaos, anarchy and dictatorship? Or the birth of a new society brought about by a revolutionary change in human nature? The

Holy Spirit is the most powerful force in the world today. Man can split the atom. The Holy Spirit is uniting humanity through men who listen to Him and obey. It needs to be a daily experience. It is practical. It works.

The basic struggle is for the wills of men. That is the ideological struggle. It goes on in your heart and mine every day. Armies and pacts and economic assistance are necessary. But the deciding factor is whether as men and nations we are guided by the voice of materialism or the Voice of God.

Mackinac Island, June 1952

4

FOR ALL MEN, EVERYWHERE

FRANK BUCHMAN saw Moral Re-Armament as a programme of global change. It is for everyone, everywhere. "Any idea that leaves anybody out is too small for this age." The call to every human being is to be a remaker of the world. Nothing less, to Frank Buchman, matched the claims of God on a man's life.

In this task, God will guide everyone who is ready to enlist. The Holy Spirit, Buchman never tired of saying, is the greatest force in the world today, directing the lives of all who listen and obey. "That is the force we ought to study."

During the years covered by these final speeches, Frank Buchman, who was seventy-five in 1953, travelled to India, Ceylon, Kashmir and Pakistan (taking a task force of 200 people with him), to Egypt, Iran and Turkey, to Australia, New Zealand, the Philippines, Japan, Viet-Nam, Thailand, Burma, Egypt and Morocco, as well as the United States and Canada, and the countries of Europe. He particularly cherished his lifelong links with countries in Asia, and counted among his friends many of the statesmen as well as a host of other men and women from these lands.

In 1950, Robert Schuman wrote the foreword to the French edition of his speeches. Schuman was Foreign Minister of France, later Prime Minister and author of the Schuman Plan. He wrote: "If we were being presented with some new scheme for the public welfare or another theory I should be sceptical. But what Moral Re-Armament brings us is a philosophy of life applied in action . . . the beginning of a far-reaching transformation of society in which the first steps have already been made."

Bread, hope, peace

Men are hungry for bread, for peace, and for the hope of a new world order.

Before a God-led unity every last problem will be solved. Hands will be filled with work, stomachs with food, and empty hearts with an ideology that really satisfies. That is what Moral Re-Armament is out for. It gives faith to the faithless, but also helps men of faith to live so compellingly that cities and nations change.

A nation where everyone cares enough and everyone shares enough, so that everyone has enough, will pattern a new social and economic order for this and all future generations.

A nation at peace within itself will bring peace to the world.

A nation which makes *what is right* regnant in personal, industrial, political and national life will pioneer the next historic step of progress and destiny for all mankind.

New Delhi, January 1953
from an address to both houses of the
Indian parliament

The new statesmanship to end confusion

People don't seem to see eye to eye. It is so difficult for them to have a common mind. They have their own ideas and are prone to push them on others. And to begin to think of a new statesmanship that will end confusion will demand a history-making decision.

We lack a mighty positive programme which can win all men and all nations. We produce a myriad conferences and schemes that add nothing to the solution of our problems. Leaders are prone to do it in their own selfish way. They say it is for the good of the country, but it is mostly for the good of themselves, and that is the reason they miss the bus.

But there is a new statesmanship abroad in the world. Conferences which give this great positive have the cure.

Last October in Colombo an experienced United Nations diplomat attended a Moral Re-Armament Assembly of Asian and Pacific nations. He said, "I have seen more true unity and peace produced here in two weeks than in all my years at Lake Success."

I am just back from seven months in the East. A force of 200 from twenty-five countries travelled with me. We took this messsage to Ceylon, India, Kashmir and Pakistan. We were honoured guests in Egypt, Iran and Turkey. One thing is certain. These countries are united in their response to Moral Re-Armament.

It was Jinnah, the founder of Pakistan, who invited me to his country. On the one free night he had in London, he went to see our play *The Forgotten Factor*. He came tired and worn after a busy day, feeling he had not reached his objectives. He sat in silence until a line in the play described the hard-headed industrialist who would not change his mind, in these words, "Will not budge." Jinnah laughed, and from then on he was living in a new climate. He came to my home afterwards for dinner and said, "I want you in Pakistan. You have the answer to the hates of the world. Honest apology—that is the golden key." Those were Mr. Jinnah's words.

But who will put that key into the lock of history and open the gates of the future for all men everywhere to enjoy peace on this earth?

In my lifetime I have seen two history-making discoveries. The discovery of the *atom* as a source of untold energy and its mobilisation. That has given us the atomic age. The other discovery is of *man* as the source of untold energy and his mobilisation. That has given us the ideological age. It is the key to events around us.

While statesmen plan for armies and conferences and alliances, the disruptive forces win a dock worker, a civil servant, a scientist, a soldier, a schoolteacher. They mobilise the grievances, the bitterness, the righteous longings for a better world in the hearts of these men. They set them on the march with a total commitment to capture the world with their idea. So while Cabinets call for more production, there are 'slow-downs' in industry. While statesmen call for another conference, vital secrets are betrayed. While everyone calls for unity between nations, disunity grows within nations.

What is the answer? The statesmanship which can set the ordinary man on the march with a vision, comradeship and plan to remake the world.

Sometimes we are tempted to wonder if there is another way. Everyone in every nation seems to have his own solution based on personal and national advantage. But the secret is, "Not my way, but God's way. Not my will, but God's will."

This is the cure for confusion—making God the decisive authority—not saying "Yes" with our lips only, but also with the discipline of our lives. It makes you natural, it makes you real. You need never try to appear wiser or better than you really are. This is the sort of person people will flock to and follow.

Confusion comes from compromise. Clarity comes from change. The moral change that illumines the darkest motives and mobilises the latent powers. If only we could see our nations as others see us, then we would want to change.

Absolute moral standards are the well-spring of inspired statesmanship. We talk of peace and unity, but forget that no man who harbours ill-will can solve the hates of nations. We criticise stubbornness in others, but ignore the selfwill which our children are so familiar with in ourselves. We talk of divine guidance, but forget that it is the pure in heart who see God. It is not those who talk, but those who listen who receive guidance. The key to new statesmanship is new statesmen.

This is my seventy-fifth birthday. I have long experience in many lands. It all comes back to basic moral truth, to absolute honesty, absolute purity, absolute unselfishness and absolute love, to the guidance of God and the total commitment to His Will. Without that experience we have nothing. With it, we have everything. A new world spelt out in new men. That is our only hope. The evidence is conclusive.

London, June 1953
following his visit to Asia and the
Middle East

The electronics of the spirit

I found something new in Los Angeles.

I found it at a dinner.

And I found it in a man. He is a pioneer of the new science of electronics which is leading us into an age beyond the atom age.

Now electronics is a new science. Spirit has been known for a long time. It's an old science. But linked with electronics, it hitches the world to a new dimension of life and thought. Millions can speedily, automatically yield to this new practice, the Electronics of the Spirit.

We can scarcely grasp what the Electronics of the Spirit means. We just faintly glimpse it. Think of the veritable instantaneous reaction whereby a thought can travel across America in less than one-fiftieth of a second. And now, with electronics, in a flash you not only hear the voice but the time you speak is registered and you get the bill at the end of the month, all without any human aid. No words of mine can explain it.

Then take the Electronics of the Spirit. It works with an Infinite Mind. It circles the globe instantly. It taps resources hitherto unexplored and forces hitherto unknown. Take the whole question of guidance—God's Mind and my mind. The thought that slips in any time, day or night, can be the thought of the Author of mind. We are dealing here with facts that no one can measure.

A thought comes—maybe just an arresting tick. One responds to it. And millions can be the richer if it is effectively carried out. It may apply to someone who crosses our path—some friend, perhaps, who may be the link which can reach cabinets, which can prevent nations from taking the wrong turning.

The Electronics of the Spirit is available for everyone. It is not only necessary but normal for all men everywhere. The *Afro-American*, most respected national Negro newspaper in America, caught the joy of this basic answer given at the Afro-Asian Conference with its bold headline, "Moral Re-Armament urged in Bandung." The story reads, "Dr Jamali, chairman of the Iraq delegation, speaking at the opening of the conference called for 'moral re-armament as the need of the world today'. He received a vigorous, sustained ovation." The speech concluded, "We must work on the basis of moral re-armament. The world would then turn into one integral camp with no Eastern or Western camps."

These truths are readily perceived and speedily acceptable

to the far-flung Moslem world which can be a girder of unity for all civilisation. My ancestor, the scholar Bibliander, was the first man to make the riches of the Koran available for Europe when he translated it into German 413 years ago. Today the Secretary-General of the Arab League says, "The Arab world hails the advent of Moral Re-Armament as one of the most significant factors on the world scene."

The Prime Minister of Egypt, in a message to the Washington Assembly for Moral Re-Armament early this year, said, "The problems of government which confront the statesmen will not be solved without this secret of a change of heart which you are giving back to the world. It will lift men everywhere above the hates and jealousies fostered by selfish interest and recall them to the creative inspiration which comes from obedience to the Will of God."

We have reached a point where man must either solve his problems or be destroyed by them. Politicians in every country are beginning to discover that the human mind, however able and sincere, cannot solve the problems created by the human passions of hate and greed and fear. It needs an electronic intervention, an experience of the Spirit. It needs the new dimension that can usher in a new age. This experience must go into every department of life in every land.

How to catch this new dimension? St Francis of Sales says the secret is to listen to the inner voice. He says that half an hour a day is a basic minimum, except when you are exceptionally busy. Then a full hour is necessary.

An Italian priest declares that writing down the thoughts which come from the Mind of God to the mind of man is advisable. He says, "What you do not write down, you will forget. So you might as well never have thought it." He adds that we reach the Presence of God when and only when our wills are touched and crossed.

The Electronics of the Spirit, so simple, so natural, and so fundamental. Herein lies the key to a new age.

Statesmanship without the Electronics of the Spirit, without guidance and without change, is like flying an aircraft in stormy weather over uncharted territory without choosing to use radio, maps or compass. It is both unnecessary and criminal. It is recklessly selfish. It leads inevitably to disaster.

With the Electronics of the Spirit, renaissance becomes inevitable—and it can happen fast. The statesman, the business man, the labour leader, the workers, the housewife, the family—all have their part to play. Guided by God, all can build unity and answer the frustrations and divisions of our times. The Electronics of the Spirit holds the answer to the second half of the twentieth century.

It is an answer that works.

Mackinac Island, May 1956

The wrong way and the right way

"We are not ready to live in the world that faces us." The man who says this is a production genius in charge of 400 scientists and 35,000 men who launched Atlas in answer to Sputnik. There is a wrong way and a right way of launching a rocket into space. There is a wrong way and a right way of living on earth.

We have been living the wrong way for so long that we have come to accept it as normal. Broken homes, disrupted industries, divided nations, deadlocked conferences—these things are not normal. They are the inevitable outcome of doing things the wrong way. Many people condemn Communism. But could it be that the hate, greed, fear and selfishness which create confusion and division in our own society, are the strength and essence of Communism? Millions who would never join the Communist Party, make its advance inevitable by the way they live.

The right way is not "my way". It may not even be "your way". The right way is God's way. Some seem to think that freedom and democracy mean "do as you please". Each man decides and goes his own way. Fathers and mothers do as they please and then they are alarmed when their children follow their example. It is estimated that more than one million youth will go through the juvenile courts this year in America. Broken homes spread disillusion throughout the nation.

There is a wrong way and a right way in statesmanship. A high official of the German Foreign Office, former Ambassador to Canada, told the press, "The most astonishing event of post-war European politics is the reconciliation of Germany and France. A major factor in the birth of an apparently permanent friendship between these former enemies is Moral Re-Armament." And Dr Adenauer, the German Chancellor, in a letter to me says, "Unless this work of Moral Re-Armament is extended the peace of the world cannot be preserved." The Chancellor talks of Moral Re-Armament as "the unseen but effective force" in achieving international agreements.

A diplomat who has been at the heart of the great international conferences that have taken place in the last fifteen years writes to say, "Three events in recent months have amazed the diplomats." In each case the answer has been found through men who have changed.

The first was the Lebanon crisis. This issue which divided the world was solved by ten Arab nations who united to bring an answer to East and West. The man most responsible for this was the Secretary-General of the

Arab League, who was in Egypt when he heard the news of crisis. He had the compelling thought, which he believed came from God, to fly immediately to New York. He obeyed. He found the Arab States divided amongst themselves, and all the other nations divided against each other. There was a real risk of war. Early one morning a further thought came to him, that the Arab nations were meant to be a bridge and not a battleground. He brought them all together in one room, and they stayed together until they found a resolution on which they all agreed. When it was put to the United Nations, the vote was 80-0.

The Times of London said, "Overnight an almost magical transformation has come over the scene."

The second event was the new unity being brought to birth through Asia. A token of this was the visit of the President of the Philippines and his reception in the Japanese Diet. Little more than a year ago the feeling between those two countries was so intense that such an action would have been political suicide. The man who, as Speaker of the Japanese Diet, received the Philippine President, and was one of the plenipotentiaries who signed the Peace Treaty for his country, says that in the last two years Moral Re-Armament has brought reconciliation between Japan and the Philippines, established new relations with Indonesia and Viet-Nam, ended a dispute with Free China, and is now in the process of healing the division between South Korea and his country. The President of the Philippines says, "The bitterness of former years is being washed away by compassion and forgiveness." The *New York World-Telegram* comments, "This visit of the President of the Philippines to Japan may mark an historic turning point in post-war affairs."

The third most recent event is the Cyprus settlement. An Asian Ambassador in Washington was in my home. He had been chairman of the committee that vainly tried to bring an answer to Cyprus in the United Nations. He told us, "Cyprus unsolved would have shattered European unity and could have led to European war this year." The answer was brought by men—British, Greeks and Turks, who through Moral Re-Armament honestly faced the fact that they had been doing things the wrong way. A British Member of Parliament went to see some of the Cyprus leaders and was honest about the places where he felt he and his country had made mistakes. A Greek leader expressed his sorrow to the British leaders in London for the situation of bitterness and bloodshed in Cyprus. A Turkish editor went to Athens and in an article which appeared throughout the Greek press, said that his country and Greece were meant to live as brothers and not as enemies. The *New York Times* called it "a resounding success for enlightened statesmanship." Is not this the answer for our overworked and under-inspired statesmen?

A diplomat of world experience says, "In Africa today they are saying everywhere to the white man, 'How soon can you leave?' But to the Moral Re-Armament men and women they are saying, 'How soon can you come?' "

The newspaper of Ibadan, the great Nigerian city where the largest university in West Africa is situated, came out with the headline, "MRA is our only hope."

In the great cities of South Africa *Freedom* has been showing to packed audiences. In Cape Town the manager of the theatre himself introduced the film and said, "We believe this is the most effective weapon in the free countries today to win the world to the right idea." At the end of the film the man who plays the part of the Prime Minister in it, the former President of the African teachers of South Africa, steps in front of the screen in the glorious robes which he wears in *Freedom*. He speaks to those audiences, which is an unprecedented event in the life of South Africa. For probably all the white people in that theatre it is the first time they have ever listened to an African speaking. Afterwards night after night he is surrounded by those who want to find from him the secret of how to get their own lives and the life of South Africa on the right way.

A battle is being fought for the mind of the world. Think of the mothers in Asia, Europe, Africa, yes, even America, who weep because their children are learning the wrong way to live from the motion pictures we make in the West. Rickard Tegström, the brilliant Walt Disney cameraman, who went to Africa to film *Freedom*, spoke of the films he saw in Africa. He says, "From white screens against the blue-black African night, the dregs of Western civilisation's film production were poured out over defenceless young Africans night after night." Now this cameraman is lending his genius to put the answer on celluloid. He is at present completing the filming of *The Crowning Experience*. It is inspired by the marvel of the life of Mary McLeod Bethune, born of slave parents, who rose to be the adviser of Presidents in the White House, and who said of Moral Re-Armament, "To be a part of this great uniting force of our age, is the crowning experience of my life."

The Crowning Experience showed in the South as a play for four months last year and then broke the 123-year attendance record at the National Theatre in Washington. Of its effect a leading newspaperman of Atlanta said, "This is the greatest news story to come out of the South this year." Rickard Tegström adds, "Filming must be in the hands of men who understand the need of the world today and the deepest need of mankind. The statesmen who realise this in time can save the world from disaster."

That's it. The whole-hearted, single-minded, completely dedicated commitment to provide our nations with leaders who are fear-free, hate-free, greed-free, men and women who know the strategy, the power and the unity that comes when the will is totally given to God for the building of a new world.

There is a wrong way and a right way for statesmanship. MRA has conclusively demonstrated in some of the most critical national and international deadlocks that when the fear, hate and greed in man is changed, solutions are rapidly achieved. This is the panorama before us—so simple that many miss it, so fundamental we cannot do without it.

Mackinac Island, June 1959

Brave men choose

Forty years ago this month there came to Oxford a man who had some knowledge of life, some insight into the ways of East and West, who had spent days with Gandhi in India and Sun Yat-Sen in China. In what is now Kerala he met an English bishop who said: "You must go to Oxford. They need the experience you have found."

During those forty years, the conviction he brought to Oxford has been a live issue, rousing men and nations through those who have chosen or rejected his challenge.

It was an Oxford man, a Member of Parliament for twenty-five years, a man who played a part in the Cyprus settlement, who this week spoke up for this conviction in public debate. A week before, the head of a College spoke boldly of it in introducing that great African film, *Freedom*, to an Oxford audience. These men, and many others, are in the line of those who in Britain's history have brought integrity into national life by their decision. The title of this speech, *Brave Men Choose*, is taken from a book by an Oxford man on this very theme, that brave men turn the course of history.

One such man in Oxford was Professor Streeter. The message rang a clarion call to this great scholar. It challenged him. It touched him. In Oxford Town Hall, before many members of the University, he said: "I have been watching this work with what diplomatists call 'benevolent neutrality.' Tonight I have decided . . . During these last years I have felt the world situation becoming more full of depression, more full of despair. There is a great deal of goodwill, but there is not enough of it to solve our tremendous problems—war, class-war and economic breakdown." Later he said: "Modern civilisation can only be saved by a moral awakening. It can happen in Britain. It will happen if those who lead Britain learn to find in God their inspiration and direction. And Britain thus led would save the world."

"I have decided." There is the key.

It was another great Oxford man, the late Marquess of Salisbury who, speaking in the House of Lords, said: "The cause of the world's state is not economic. The cause is moral." He echoed Dr Streeter's conviction when he said: "If I may use a phrase which is common in a great movement taking place at this moment in this country and elsewhere, what you want are God-guided personalities, which make God-guided nationalities, to make a new world. All other ideas of economic adjustment are too small really to touch the centre of the evil."

In East London, in the cradle of the British Labour movement, where Moral Re-Armament was launched, there were also brave men who chose. There was Tod Sloan, Keir Hardie's fellow fighter from the docks. He wrote: "Chaos cannot obtain if we work, live and practise Moral Re-Armament. It is a real laughing, living, loving obedient willingness to restore God to leadership. This to me is the only revolution that matters—the change of human nature—and it does happen."

There was Ben Tillett, pioneer of the dockers' unions across the world. From his deathbed he sent this word, "Tell Frank Buchman to go on fighting. You have a great international movement. Use it. It is the hope of tomorrow. It will bring sanity back to the world."

The Earl of Athlone, who first met this message in 1929 when he was Governor-General of South Africa, speaking in a radio broadcast to the British Commonwealth in the early days of the war, said: "The call for Moral Re-Armament has encircled the world, and become a source of fresh hope to millions of men and women. Heads of States, national, civic and industrial leaders of all classes, creeds and parties have welcomed it as the cure for that deep disease of the spirit from which civilisation is suffering.

"Moral Re-Armament stands for a change of heart, for that new spirit which must animate all human relationships. It calls on us to make the will of God the guiding force, as for individuals, so for homes and nations."

As the ideological struggle intensified across the world, a growing multitude caught the fire of these pioneers. For only men ablaze for the right can ever hope today to win men who burn for the wrong. "Fire from heaven", that is how Don Sturzo, patriot-priest of Italy, described Moral Re-Armament in a message sent to the World Assembly on Mackinac Island. His thinking inspired the Christian Democrat parties of Italy, France and Germany, which have given three great Europeans to the world— Prime Minister de Gasperi, Prime Minister Schuman and Chancellor Adenauer.

Prime Minister de Gasperi expressed his conviction that Moral Re-Armament by going "to the root of the world's evils will bring about the understanding between men and nations for which all people long."

Prime Minister Schuman wrote: "What Moral Re-Armament brings us is a philosophy of life applied in action. It is not a question of a change of policy. It is a question of changing men. Democracy and her freedoms can be saved only by the quality of the men who speak in her name."

Chancellor Adenauer knows the value of Moral Re-Armament. He says it has played "an unseen but effective part in bridging differences of opinion between negotiating parties in important international agreements."

These brave men chose. Now a world-wide army is surging forward on every continent.

This is the word of a man on his eighty-third birthday who has spent a long life up and down the world meeting and knowing men.

It is the word of a man who has known the personal friendship of viceroys and governors of India and of the men who opposed them, and brought them together; who knows the problems of Africa at first hand since 1929, and these statesmen of Europe and the Americas for more than fifty years. He has seen the development of two materialist ideologies and the devastation of two world wars, the retreat of freedom, and now the advance of a mighty answer.

We are facing world revolution. There are only three possibilities open to us. We can give in, and some are ready to do just that. Or we can fight it out, and that means the risk of global suicide. Or we can find a superior ideology that shows the next step ahead for the Communist and the non-Communist world alike. What we shall never do effectively is to patch things up by pretending that basic differences do not exist or do not matter, or by supposing that an ideological challenge can be met by economic, political or military means alone. Absolute moral standards are not just questions of individual conduct today. They are the conditions of national survival. We need to scour out the dirt in our national life, our political life, our economic life, our school life and our home life through a change in men. Wherever men give man the place in their lives that God alone should have, slavery has begun. "Men must choose to be governed by God, or they condemn themselves to be ruled by tyrants".

There is no neutrality in the battle between good and evil. No nation can be saved on the cheap. It will take the best of our lives and the flower of our nations to save humanity. If we go all-out for God we will win.

Then it is the brave man chooses,
While the coward stands aside,
Till the multitude make virtue
Of the faith they had denied.

Caux, June 1961
Frank Buchman's last speech on his
eighty-third birthday, a few weeks before
he died in August 1961

FRANK BUCHMAN

By Peter Howard

Frank Buchman is an American of distinguished Swiss descent. One of his ancestors was the successor to Zwingli in Zürich and translator of the Koran into German. After his family came to America in 1740 they settled in Pennsylvania. One ancestor fought with Washington at Valley Forge. Another was the first man to enlist in Abraham Lincoln's army during the war between the States.

In the year 1921 Frank Buchman was invited by a British military adviser to join him at Washington during the Disarmament Conference. It was a significant occasion for two reasons. First, because on the train to Washington the impelling thought filled Buchman's mind, "Resign, resign, resign!" He faced the moral challenge to be willing to abandon the financial security and comfort of a salaried position for an unknown road. Second, because the Conference sessions confirmed his conviction that plans for world peace were inadequate unless they reckoned with the necessity of a change in human nature.

Soon he was enlisting and training people of every stratum of society to bring to their nations a basic change in economic, social, national and international relationships, all stemming from personal change. Within a few years, through the impact of a returning group of Rhodes Scholars who had met him in Oxford University, Buchman's work was to acquire nationwide significance in South Africa. The Press of that country first bestowed on his friends the title of "The Oxford Group".

The work spread rapidly. By the 'thirties it had become world-wide. Norway's delegate at Geneva, later to become President of the League of Nations, said: "Where we have failed in changing politics, you have succeeded in changing lives, and given men and women a new way of living."

In 1938, realistically facing the fact that armed conflict could not finally decide the ideological issue in the world, Buchman launched the programme of Moral Re-Armament which stated the need of moral force to win a war and to build a just peace.

Frank Buchman's insight and action began to stir the nations to prepare for the ideological conflict. This was precisely what the Fascists and Communists feared most, that to the industrial and armed might of the democracies should be added the superforce of an inspired ideology.

From the beginning he was heavily attacked by all who did not wish to see a moral ideology take root in the world. The Communist attacks were based on the usual technique of calling anyone they feared a Fascist. The Nazis said that his work "supplies the Christian garment for world democratic aims . . . It is clearly opposed to National Socialism."

Today when events have been successively proving the rightness of Buchman's ideological insight, while continuing to stress the danger of Communism he has increasingly emphasised that anti-Communism is not a cure. The answer, he says, lies in a moral and spiritual ideology adequate to cure the moral weaknesses of our civilisation and creative enough to win the allegiance of masses of people in every land who justifiably look for change.

Although statesmen have sought his aid, sometimes publicly and more often privately, although he is humanly speaking the leader of a major world force, yet Buchman has never lost his humour, and his unique caring for individuals and their needs has grown through the years.

In this task of remaking the world to which he has dedicated himself he has shown another great quality rare in our time, of developing and training others to take responsibility. He often says, "You have never succeeded unless you have trained ten men to do your work better than you can do it yourself." The continuance of his life work is secured for the future by the principle of revolutionary teamwork.

His love for people, his sensitiveness to their needs and failures, his gift for creating in them the will to live their best, is an art. It is the secret of the growth of his work. It is an art which he says can be normal for every man. A Scottish miner, Peter O'Connor, said of an interview with Frank Buchman: "In my half-hour with you I was helped more than by any other living soul." To which Buchman commented, "It was not my art. It is God's art."

Since engaging on this work thirty years ago Buchman has never had a permanent home. His force of fully trained personnel is in the hundreds. They work without salary, yet they never go hungry. Says Frank Buchman of this fact, "Where God guides, He provides."

Thousands of people, convinced of the basic necessity of this answer, sacrifice to advance this revolutionary force. There have rarely been large gifts. There have been thousands of small gifts not from surplus, but from sacrifice. From the early days Frank Buchman's work had advanced through the sacrifices of those who believe in it. Men offer for the faith they hold most dear the things they count most precious. People have given of their wages, their capital, their houses, their savings.

In Britain, for example, dockers, miners and shop stewards in many parts of the country have formed fighting funds.

A former European Communist, asked whether industrialists contributed to the funds of Moral Re-Armament, replied: "Some do. I wish more did. Every worker should rejoice when businessmen begin to invest in a force that is fighting effectively for social justice and a new world order."

Frank Buchman is a man with a host of friends across the world.

Typical is this letter from a changed veteran Communist leader in the Ruhr, twenty-five years a member of the Party until he met Frank Buchman:

"The fight is tough but it is a fine thing, and I am grateful to be able to be in it with my family. The Good must conquer. All my spare time I spend in talking with people about this ideology and also, as well as I can, I try to live as an example of it. I have many human mistakes and weaknesses to overcome, and my family also. God has to help us time and time again. But of one thing I am certain, I have never been so happy and so contented as I am today. That I owe to you.

"Now I must stop this pen-work and give you warmest greetings from all my family, which consists of myself, my wife, my daughter and my son-in-law. At the same time I wish you the best of health.

"But above all I wish success to this wonderful ideology in all lands, so that mankind can once again become happy."

From *The World Rebuilt* by
Peter Howard, 1951

There was a secret in Frank Buchman's life.

It brought him love and hate. It led him to believe that everyone he met, rich and poor, black and white, boss and worker, could and should be made new. It bore him to the heart of nations.

It made him think and live in global terms. The last

challenge he gave, a few hours before he died, was, "I want to see the world governed by men governed by God. Why not let God run the whole world?" Forty-five years before, in 1916, he was telling a group of men and women, who did not fully understand what he was saying, "I want you to live for continents. I want you to think for continents."

People will never understand the secret of Frank Buchman unless they judge him as a revolutionary. That is what he was. He did not look at life or people through the same eyes as those of other men. He did not think of people as black, white, brown or yellow, but as sons of God with the same needs which the same answer could meet. He said, "It is not a question of colour, but of character." And in 1915, on the first of his nine visits to Asia, he said, "Crows are black the whole world over", meaning that human nature is everywhere the same.

He did not think that a man was a better or worse man because of his wealth—or lack of it. He sympathized with poor men and did his best to help them materially and in every way—but he was far from that patronage of poverty which refuses to face the need of the poor for the same honesty and purity that the world rightly demands from the rich. Challenged once that Moral Re-Armament was a "class movement", he replied instantly, "That is so. We believe there are two classes in the world—men who change and those who refuse to do so."

He said, "There is enough in the world for everybody's need but not for everybody's greed. If everybody cared enough, and everybody shared enough, wouldn't everybody have enough?"

A diplomat who, for a quarter of a century, has had to negotiate with the Russians and others at most of the post-war conferences, gave this verdict on Buchman: "He has done three things. He saw the real problem many years before the rest of us understood it. He forged an answer out of human lives that cured the problem. He then did the hardest job of all—he built a force of people in every continent who are bringing that answer to the world."

Mark Twain used to say that what troubled him in the Bible was not the parts he did not understand, but the parts that he did. That is true, for many, of Frank Buchman's work.

He undertook the task of changing the trend of his time. The head of an Oxford College said, in the summer of 1961, that people no longer discuss whether or not to live moral standards: the truth is that nowadays millions believe that neither right nor wrong exists.

In the midst of all this, Buchman for half-a-century strode fearlessly forward, proclaiming old truths in new ways, facing decadent generations with a decision to let God clean up themselves and their nations from top to bottom. He challenged the statesman and the ordinary man with standards which, if accepted, mean revolution in all they think and do. In the landslide of morality and the shifting sands of an age of licence, he gave the solid rock of eternal values and truth.

Of course he was persecuted. Men with such a message have been persecuted all through the ages. Some self-styled Christians who compromise on divorce, sex, drink, gambling, money and Communism, forget that Christ was crucified by the pious of his day—not because he was wrong but because he was right. How many Christians today draw any clear moral line through a community?

Buchman never shared the views of those who present Christ as powerless to cure the sickness of sin in a man or in a continent. He felt that powerless Christians were a denial of the Master they professed to serve.

He won the loyalty and love of a host of friends. By

others he was hated, sneered at, lied about, mocked and scoffed at—and he was right. Some of his enemies continued their dance of derision upon his grave. They will not disturb his rest.

He used to say, "Persecution is the fire that forges prophets. Stones of criticism are so bracing. They just set you up for the day."

His answer was the conviction that "an extreme of evil must be met with an extreme of good. A fanatical following of evil by a passionate pursuit of good. Only a passion can cure a passion. And only a superior world-arching ideology can cure a world divided by warring ideologies."

His was an heroic march at a time when moral courage is rarer than it used to be. "Unto us may grace be given to follow in his train."

At a time of crisis the only sane thing is to change people.

Buchman lived his life in the faith and experience that human nature, starting with his own, could be changed. That was the root of the answer.

When men change, national economies change. That is the fruit of the answer.

With a crescendo of changed lives, world history can be changed. That, he said, was the destiny of our age.

The world talks about peace, but prepares for war. Buchman saw that peace was not just an idea, but people becoming different, and that the true peace-makers were those willing to pay the price of it by giving their lives to bring millions under God's control. That was his life and his secret.

From *Frank Buchman's Secret*,
by Peter Howard, 1961

FOR FURTHER READING

REMAKING THE WORLD, The Collected Speeches of Dr. Frank N. D. Buchman, with an introduction by Alan Thornhill, Blandford Press, London, 1961.

FRANK BUCHMAN'S SECRET, by Peter Howard, Heinemann, London, 1961.

PETER HOWARD, LIFE AND LETTERS, by Anne Wolrige Gordon, Hodder and Stoughton, London, 1969.

DYNAMIK AUS DER STILLE, *Die Aktualität Frank Buchmans*, by Theophil Spoerri, former Rector of the University of Zurich and Professor of French and Italian literature, *Caux Verlag*, Lucerne, 1971; also published in French, *La dynamique du silence*, *Editions de Caux*, Lucerne, 1972; English edition in preparation.

EXPERIMENT WITH GOD, *Frank Buchman Rediscovered*, by Gösta Ekman, religious editor of Svenska Dagbladet, Hodder and Stoughton, London, 1972.

GOOD GOD, IT WORKS! by Garth Lean, Blandford Press, London, 1974.

FRANK BUCHMAN AS I KNEW HIM, by H. W. "Bunny" Austin, Grosvenor Books, London, 1975.

From your bookseller, or from the MRA Bookshop, 12, Palace Street, London, SW1E 5JF.
Please write for the current lists of books and pamphlets, plays, records, films, and details of NEW WORLD NEWS, published weekly.